fancy beasts

ALSO BY ALEX LEMON

Happy: A Memoir

Hallelujah Blackout

Mosquito

fancy

POEMS

beasts

ALEX LEMON

MILKWEED EDITIONS

Published 2010 by Milkweed Editions
Printed in Canada
Cover and interior design by Christian Fuenfhausen
Cover image by Custom Creature Taxidermy Arts.
©2009 Sarina Brewer
The text of this book is set in Fairfield LH.
10 11 12 13 14 5 4 3 2 1
First Edition

Please turn to the back of this book for a list of the
sustaining funders of Milkweed Editions.

Library of Congress Cataloging-in-Publication Data

Lemon, Alex.
  Fancy beasts : poems / Alex Lemon. — 1st ed.
    p. cm.
  ISBN 978-1-57131-443-7 (pbk. with flaps : alk. paper)
  I. Title.
  PS3612.E468F36 2010
  811'.6—dc22
                                    2009040445

This book is printed on acid-free paper.

FOR ARIANE

come sweetly

It starts
The way

It ends—
Fingers of

Impossible light
Crawling

Over your
Face. In

Between—mind-
Less waiting.

Mouth gunk
Or a gunked

Up heart—
Going is just

Climbing
Back inside.

!

Jesus is dead, Marx is dead, Elvis is dead
And I'm not feeling too good myself

—A T-SHIRT IN SANTA MONICA

being here

Listless blight, safe words, every little
Sound in the night is a gasp—bone tip

Blossoming through skin. It's no
Bull, man. Anymore, we're all winners

& afraid to pull these faces off.
Maple leaves & plastic bags somersault

Through the park. One cloud
Grips the moon. Call me anything

Before morning comes, little lover,
Because it's true & doesn't fucking matter.

Kill the lights. Feel the burn. Rev yourself
Up & sing along with the good thrum

Found in everything. Hang around
Until the end. Melt my ashes on your tongue.

all of the
made roads

Choosing
My life, I drop

Quarters in
The slot

& select
The worst

Song on
The jukebox

& then sneak
Out to

Watch
Through the rain-

Streaked glass.
O feverish

Praise—I can
Feel night

Struggle
To lay

Back in
Its own dark.

way out west

A hard rain will show the secret
In the architecture of bones
Much better than sunlight believe me
Or fractures I promise you
So soaked T-shirts drip like a true skin
While we walk laughing
Down the beach & after the drops stop
Pocking the water the tricks
That play on the growing green then
Bluer waves   O blackshark & tigerbelly
Out there   Believe me   How I wish
I could wrap everything I see
In cellophane & keep it forever in the freezer
This fizzing pier life   Arches painted
In a crown of muscle men & clown faces
Red coral lips & russet mustaches
All the finest whisperings of deeper-than-just-flesh
Each sunset something out there
On the horizon looks like it's waving
An arm going under & down   Vanishing
Into the watery sweep   & even in
The complete black after
Everything's slipped from the world's shelf
A sort of gravelly piano rails
Over the palm tree's hidden speakers & though I know
Some things believe me
They are so few & stars are burning

Mouths in the sky   Believe
Me & the desolation of legs outlined
By a wet blue skirt leave
Never enough time to explain

ghost in the latrine

If the choice between
The men's & women's

Restroom decides
Your identity, what does

The man playing air guitar
With a tennis racket

In front of the urinals
Have to do with Lacan?

I thought it was Larry Craig,
But he turned around & it was

Craig Mack that slapped me
& said that this was his

House. It was a thousand degrees
Beneath the sink lights.

I wanted to ask why
He was in the ladies'

Room, but the twists
In my gut froze me.

Razzmatazz slopped
Across the tiles. My life

Story appeared in the mirror
Steam when he stormed

Out. I don't remember
There being such a dearth

Of good music, so many
Apples gonging on tin roofs.

more wind

I watch the beautiful
Charity of a body peeling,

The heart floating
In a bathtub for hours

Before sinking to the reddy
Bottom. Sing, *I love you*

Like the sea-salty kiss
Of death while toweling

Off & my finger will rap
The window glass. I swear

My intentions are pure—
But damn—those bags

Under your eyes are
Dynamite. What kind

Of hotness are you smuggling

In there? I'm too brittle
For Twister, so come on,

Let's play spin the neuroses.
I swear there won't be any tie 'em

Up & spank spank. Not one
Second of Boggle, I promise.

Out here it's the land of the free.
Home of the craven.

Come out, come out—
Show me what you can

Do with a dozen skunks
Nailed to a dead man.

it had only been dead
a few hours

What a strange paradise this is—
languid apricot trees & birds

of paradise. Tire-flattened
oranges in the alley & ants

in the hummingbird feeders.
Neighbors peek from the blinds

when the sprinklers torque on
& I cannot romanticize this

ultimate torture test. You say
your foot is killing you?—well,

hot damn, you are dead
nuts, right on. That is the essence

of all of this, isn't it? So let me tell you—
they begin as piles of bones,

the animals in my dreams do.
Each night, they clink & clonk

& rise like a time-lapse video
of skyscraper construction.

One animal turns into a man
& the man gives birth

to a dead dog. In just seconds
the other animals have rent them apart

& then, I'm awake. Night swallows
knife through the morning

fog as I stand at the window
listening to the coyote song.

My entire body is killing me,
& I have witnessed my own death

& lived—I whisper my wagers
against disaster into the dark air.

haunt

In the beginning there was
the beginning there was bafflement
in the beginning there was
in the beginning the bewildered
asking questions *you've got to be kidding*
there was bafflement in the eyes in
the beginning & then in the beginning
there was blood in the mouth there was blood
there the blood was thimblefuls & cups
& then whole slopping rivers
baffled & bewildered in the beginning
with footsmears of blood the train tracks & song
all baffling lines of clouds never moving & what waves
from the backseat of cars that little hand
that wonders what it means to have your face
scalped neatly away & hung in a loose mask
over the back of your skull the
grotesqueries of this place can you imagine
wearing such a bloody thing what happened
to the beginning? the bodies of murdered children
are dumped at the edge of town oh
it's time lord everyone must go

the floppy instant

FOR MA

I felt like I was
In the presence

Of dynamite,
Deserving of

Everything. Outside,
The hallway bubbled—

Travelers realizing
They had something

Better in mind.
It is the human

Situation, stewing
& bewildered

With insignificance.
There's a vastness

Of form & content
In airports that can

Only be bridged
By a complex

Framework of hatreds
That herald the dark.

There is something I love
About the wolves lying

In wait. I am a friend
Of the animals.

here comes the mojo

The theme of this place is
Go big & sloppy. So call me

Back & let's cuddle. We've got to get
This thing started. Let's spoon until

It goes dark. Until our organs
Are cut out of prone, bathtub-

Cradled bodies. A jack-in-the-box
On the toilet. Long for what you

Always find in your pockets instead
Of flinching when your shrunken

Head springs out of the toy box
Like a sock monkey. Stop, drop

& roll doesn't work because you can't
Feel your body. The shower spits on.

Vomit clogs the drain. Oh how it changes
Everything—this kind of kingliness.

Let yourself feel it. Let it come
Down. You are the amphetamine

& midnight Vegas type
Of Elvis. Mad eyed & hip shaking—

Cherry, cherry, spin—gimme
Gimme that jackpot of believing.

california hates you

The golden rat reclines & gnaws on the aloe
   plant with the sky empty of clouds this

day just like yesterday & the one before it if you
   think I'm going to cum with the curtains

not open you don't know me at all my breath taken
   away it is a shame we have to say good-bye

every seven years to our old flesh all those jackets
   of flaking skin my closet is filled with them

the blurry year of sunlight making the last one rough
   as corduroy like bacon like turned & dried out

garden dirt instead it might be nice if the layers piled
   & grew atop each other so the world's weight

might be something shoulderable something to shift
   to the other arm as you whoosh open

your enormous umbrella when the deluge starts
   purpledark & splatting the sidewalk on down

beautification campaign

Liposuction for everyone who can recite
the Pledge of Allegiance! Lip gloss, Lee
Press-On Nails arrive weekly in the mail.
The turkey is always fat free & the cottage
cheese is nothing but protein. Helicopters
drop leaflets, but in truth, no one understands
the food pyramid. & so I'm inconsolable—
I can't get rid of these love handles. The woman
in the radio tells me to eat more hearts
of palm but I don't know
what they look like. Bundles of skin-
tight tracksuits are thrown on each stoop
like the morning paper & I think gastric
bypass is the answer for me. I stay up late
& cut out coupons for Botox injections,
but there's no money left, so I whiten
my teeth with bleach. I toss & turn in the middle
of the night, listening to Wide-Awake Sammy
riffle through the trash outside. He doesn't sleep
& I can't stop thinking about my love
handles. When I turn the kitchen light on,
I can see him out there—filling his bag
with recyclables, his belly with whatever drops
from the half-empty cans. At the table, I fondle
my love handles & tell the cat that I'm not afraid
of science. Cut 'em right off me and feed 'em
to the dogs. But I have to admit, I've been

disappointed—you can't taste the range
in those free-range hogs. I say let all of the beef
be beef fed. I want night vision
after eating a plate of salmon. Let the teats
of cows drip with the sweetest honey. I want
my baby spinach made with real, 100 % baby.

verde vista

Waiting in line at the post office
In Thousand Oaks, California—

I'm tapped on the shoulder
& turn to see an old man

Milky-wayed with liver spots,
Skin hanging from his cheeks

Like pancake batter. *Those
Real?* he asks, pointing

At the tattoos covering my arms.
He smiles when I nod—says,

*You know, Hitler would have
Made a lamp out of you.*

He did that, you know? He
Laughs. I shake my head *yeah*

But as I start to speak, to tell him
About the one-of-a-kind baseball mitt

I played with in college—a real
Beauty & all of it sewn

From the saddle-soaped hides
Of big-mouthed elderly men,

How if I spit a bit of tobacco juice
Into the pocket, it was the kind

Of glove that wouldn't let me make
An error—the line pushes forward

& it's my turn, so I wish him a good
Day & drop my envelopes

On the counter, where a too-chipper
Man asks if I would like to purchase

A coil of the brand-new American
Flag stamps. I buy the stamps. I say

Good-bye to the old man. The mall
I have to walk through to get outside

Is adorned with holiday decorations—
Trumpeting angels & walls netted

With Christmas lights. "Jingle Bells"
Plays from speakers hidden in giant

Snowflakes. In the parking lot
The gushing sprinklers flood

The concrete while a Latino
Prunes flowering azaleas & a pit bull

Begins gnawing himself apart
In my chest. I will wait for the old man

To come out so, just as he starts up
His Cadillac, I can toss a shopping cart

Through the windshield. In a half hour
I count ten women leaving the mall

Who have obviously had plastic surgery—
Basketball-sized breasts, lips like bloated

Caterpillars, cheeks stretched taut, identical
Almond eyes & one banging body—model shaped

& gorgeous—with the head of a cadaver.
Who knows how many of the men that passed

Recently had their penises enlarged.
The old man's walker scrapes the pavement.

He stops at the curb, heavy breathing, & inside
Him, I imagine his heart dropping the white

Flag of surrender. That he is about to crumple
& the next thing I know, my piled hands

Will be compressing his sternum & his lips, tender
As the crust of a burnt loaf of bread, will open

Against mine & as the air I just breathed into him
Returns, the taste of mayonnaise & his aftershave

Fills my mouth, & I realize that in the end it will
All work out, brilliant with dirt & light. Cryogenics

& biogerontology & pregnant men & clones
Of our favorite Chihuahuas. & if the old man, still

Kicking around, vigorous with his fourth
Or fifth different baboon heart growling within

Him, wants to stay up a little longer to finish
The terrific book he's reading & tugs on

The beside lamp & is illuminated by the patchwork
Of colors that had, years before, covered

My body, well, I guess, that's fine with me, too.

bling ding bling

The oven is left on all night,
so the cupcakes turn into
twelve blackened fists,
& being that we are hoodlums
& thugs, we go outside & hit
the rock-hard treats into the air
with aluminum bats, golf clubs
& tennis rackets. It's beautiful
really, watching the dark specks
rocket over the shingled roofs.
& we won't admit it when we're
caught, but of course we're aiming. All
of us know whose windows they'll smash
through. The hands that'll pluck up
the shards. A triangle of glass arrowed
upright into the hardwood floor. Glittering
in the sunlight as we laugh & jab each other
in the mouths. Glittering & upright,
like the birthday candle on your last cake.
Upright & glittering through your cataracts
& Alzheimer's. Glittering & glittering, that candle,
that last sweet, that something
      you'll never remember.

pins & needles

Black threads, outline of an oak,
Bare against the sky. The digging

Ground pulps & gasps. October is
Pregnant with grief. If Vallejo was

Born on a day when God was sick,
I was birthed into a bedroom filled

With dolls & their roll-back eyes.
The brackish stench of this place

Frays, but each day there are so many
Burials it's hard not to get used to it.

The hours brim & hang & sump. Every
Morning the heart wrenches back

Into my body. None of us have ever
Been. I find a soot-covered hummingbird

In my pocket each Thursday. When my
Hands are charred & then scraped clean

With a spoon, there is no better chalice.
If I could fly into myself, I'd wear my cape

Like a blindfold & mosey into
The bloated sunset. When you realize

You are missing something, it wasn't me.

heat

Blackened dead the avocado orchard is hollow barked & burnt

Dry husked & still there is no sleeping among the palms & my eyes

Go sunken & salty as I lean toward the sea & the slants of sunlight

That pilfer through the knurled arms the craggy dark where barking

Spiders trap quail to make their favorite cider & up above

Where hang the limbs that fall already perfectly curved for the back

Tines of rocking chairs & cribs & pipes that will smoke the air

With the scent of peaches & make me look for my uncle

When I walk across parking lots & for the lost there are plenty

Of fallen sticks to bind their legs with like splints or furnish

Their feet with small boats for later lighting because there is no

Longer anyone speaking to them kindly so now there is fire

That crackles like a voice or something to grind down to powder

For adding to thicken whatever they drink so it might

Somehow resemble food or soup or even blood it's plain to see

That most of us are crawling now giving up with our broken

Hip bones while somewhere at the center of a circle of joyous men

Who wear Hawaiian shirts the cries from the last orange tree

In California grow more muffled as each tan & unafflicted arm

Tacks to the polished branches another one-hundred dollar bill

redux

After you find your body floating
Down the river, pluck leaves

From the armpit & decide to put
It back on, sheets of rain upflame

The shore water. Branches bend,
Fingertipping the brown murk.

I will kiss all of the sincerity off
Of you, polish your eyelids with

Hot breath, the incessant fever
Of a survivor of the potato famine.

Let me be your guiding fright, your
Highway to the comfort zone.

On the bridge above, no one knows
What to do about the busted levees,

But everyone is comfortable,
Surrounded by all the crap

They bought yesterday
At Wal-Mart. A fault line

Zigzags through town.
The default setting is one

More, please. It is yes,
One more helping!

We planned to help
But forgot which day

The innocent criminal
Was being put to death.

We pretend to read
The newspaper to the blind

Because we never learned
To read. Grossly overestimate

How much we need to sleep.
If there really is a beginning

& then an everlasting struggle
To know the unknowable,

The tunnel at the other end
Will open on Thirsty Thursday.

A deep need to see it all
Differently will crack through

The bar each time someone
Strikes the eight ball. Because

You are so sad, I will give
Up my love for Lucifer.

i love you big brother

Cross my heart & hope to fry—
Everyone is doing their goddamn best

At their jobs. Raking the litter
Box. Chewing apart mushrooms.

We pronounce each syllable blah
Blah blah & vice versa—blah blah

Blah—each word announcing
How you don't really feel

Like respecting the rules
Of gravity anymore. So you decide

To sleep hanging from a doorway—
Upside down as if diving

Headfirst into the ground
& because no one you know is

Dying in a war you decide to play
Dead. You hang like a hidden fruit.

Like a hibernating bat. Bills pile
Up & the phone rings & rings. The first

Of the month your head turns
Into a pumpkin leaking blood.

Your feet become glass. It's not
Just a game, you think—

There's a gasping in your chest.

shall we be merry?

You can call them boots on the ground,
But I'm going to say leather houses filled

More with grit than bone—but big fat
Deal—only the Army & Imelda Marcos

Care about shoes. I'm sleeping in late,
Having those puckered dreams that catch

In my craw like Wal-Mart bags
In the hibiscus. The fluttering shape

In the flowers is the same as our DNA
On the hottest day of July. My eyes, oh

My pinhole-pupiled eyes. Stare into
Them & tell me what you see.

My head is a basement filled with shadows
Sitting around a table yelling *Yahtzee!*

If they catch you peeking in, tell them
I'd like my tools back & a four-egg omelet

Like the one I'm eating in each memory I have
Of Keenan. He touches a spoon to his nose

At the breakfast table & tells me
That the oven nearly swallowed me whole

The night before. That it was the funniest thing
He's ever seen, but at the same time,

He's weeping. Jason stands behind him
Strumming a guitar, & it is on fire. It is

Smoking. He sings of amputees, of bummers.
I guess that sums up what's happening

On the flickering screen in there. Look again
Right before I fall asleep & it's the sequel.

A man screws his own hand into a phone pole,
Gets mad & then screws everything around him

Until everything, everything is dead. I've passed
All of the time I had shaking incontinent

In the backyard, reaching out for things that keep
Moving right on by, leaving me to stand

In line getting more bovine & poorer
As the weight of my cataracts tug

Like the pull the man who stood
In the locker room of my college felt. Tennis

Shoes cinched, dangling from his brain-
Like scrotum until security showed up.

My political leanings on this scorched
& windless day have me sitting outside,

Staring at the golden rat in the orange
Tree & saying *howdy governor*

To the asshole that lives across the way.
If it means I don't get the extra chicken

Skin, even if it means I go to hell, I have
Found a way to be at peace with this. Welcome,

I say, put it in the hole chief. When the time
Comes, I will place all of my belongings

Into the duffel bag & get on the fucking floor.

fantasy island

It is a good lesson to learn, that utter silence
on the inside, heart floating in the body
like a bread bag in a pool. Here, everything else

sinks—gas cap, lace panties & your wedding
ring—all the way to the bottom. So put on your fancy
dress & let that look be named *the beat petunia.*

I'll shout your vital signs & vigilantly check
my blood pressure. I'll ask the grapefruit trees
what they think about punching them dudes

in they punk-ass faces. Come with me! Hold
that fleshy orb to the sky & listen! *Fools rush
in where angels fear to tread.* & then shake & listen

again. *A man can't be too careful in his choice
of enemies.* We'll waste whole years pressing
the fruit to our ears. *Well begun is half done.*

*Where did you find this man?—Is there an asshole
convention in town?* It will go on like this until we're mad
& you're conversing with the shadows your puppet hands make

on the sand. & then, with nothing to do when I'm gone
& you're surrounded by an empty beach, you'll peel
the grapefruit, slow & delicate, meticulously unraveling

one long, undulating rind. & under the peel, you
think, you hope, might be a poem, a fortune, something to help
you get through the hours. But when you look close

there is just a name printed in block letters on the pulp,
the name of your neighbor who just died. Each fruit
you peel has a new name, & sometimes you recognize

these names from the obituaries. The sun sets. The sun
rises. Oh, how you wish one useless poem would uncurl
from one of these peels. But the names pile & you start

to throw the fruit into the waves. The sun sets
& it is so hard to see. You pinch down the tree limbs
for grapefruit, but there's nothing there. There's no

more fruit. You wait for the sun to rise, but it seems to be
taking so long today. The trees are filled with darkness
& sleeping birds & you stare at the black clothesline

of a horizon, thinking there might be a blinking light
out there, something coming to save you,
but you itch. The sand chafes, burns your heels,

& you know—with all of the hookworm & sleeping
sickness, who the hell can really tell what's out there.
These days, it's difficult to know much of anything.

tick tick tick

The most troubling thing is everything. It's all happening
At the same time. Interpreting dreams while watching *Let's Make
A Deal*. Eating tofurkey & Cherry Garcia while practicing
Yoga. Happy Baby. Down Dog. The temperature drops
Sixty degrees in ten minutes. Stop signs wobble, wobble,
& then everyone is outside watching the meteor shower.
It is so contemporary of us to feel the sky pressing
Down. Copernicus was an impossible dullard & Darwin
Didn't even grind up the finch beaks before he smoked
Them. It is far too easy to get stuck, circling the roundabout,
Thinking about the reality show you wish you'd starred in.
The first & final season of *Let's Make a Baby*. The time
Has come to triumph over the oppression of our
Zippers. My finger is on the button of a machine
I've never seen before. Night sounds like an ice cube
Dropped into a hot bath. We could warn each other
About the coming windchill advisory. Tomorrow's slick roads.
It's so discouraging. Today, I ran the microwave
With nothing in it just to see it catch fire. The purple-
Lipped days are upon us but don't dwell on it for much
Longer than it takes to assemble the washable nativity set.
We all have a better place to be, right? My appointment
Started ten minutes ago. I slept through the alarm
& then the rest of my life.

there's so little to do in a hospital bed

Although tiredness whirls
All the while, the hive

Of my head shines with love.
Inside my chest, umbrellas

Open warmly—the last
Vacancy where I might

Get it right. My under-
Thighs have stopped

Bleeding. Even though
My skin has God's stamp

Of approval—*USDA Choice*—
Fear comes & the sheets

Look lightning struck.
Someone keeps panning

For gold in the toilet. Leaving
The water on. Water is running

Out. The midnight caller screams,
Anyone that sweets & sweats. If you

Don't know, now you know! It is time
To get a gun & a harem of lawyers.

The pipes are clogged & I'm going
To wear a suit sewn from chicken livers

For Halloween if I can make it
Outside by October. My nephews love

Me just as much as french fries.
Damn, it's great to be alive!

It is it is. Although it's supposed to
Keep raining, I could take you places.

Fish sandwiches. Perpetual foot rubs.
The ark is all patched up & night is only

An ever-looming coat of darkness.
Fine, I guess it's time to close this shit

Down. With this grease, I now
Pronounce everyone swine.

the new math

Check one. Check two.
Hold a mirror below the nostrils

& do the kind of math
You can't get wrong.
Four plus four equals

A white sheet large enough
To cover a football field
Packed, shoulder to shoulder,

With the dead. Next, throw
In some multiplication

& painkillers. Some
Of us are having
Heart attacks right now.

my fallow human beans

One must gird the loins
When approaching

Considerateness—that little
Gnashing beast. It might not

Cost much, but the way I see it,
We really know nothing about

Each other. Civilized schmivilized,
You can't fool me—I see

The crackhead lurking inside
You, those brass knuckles you say

Are a wedding band. My good thing
Might be your flayed body stuffed

Inside an eviscerated donkey,
So, my friend, intimacy is

Nothing but a thickening
Of discomfort. Do not expect

The door to be held for you.
A taxi cab will splash mud

On your brand-new pants.
Everyone but *you* is thinking

About how to save the mortal soul,
So respect the sacred, man.

You gotta fight for the right
To party & party for the right

To strife! Come over, let me
Prove it to you—we'll divide

The labor by chainsawing apart
One of my old ladies. & if the kids

Aren't done hand-sewing that new
Batch of shoes, we'll whip them real good.

!!

Not without infinite scruple would I touch anything of this.

—SIMONE WEIL

Alarm clock
& voice.

My skeleton
Is being

Absorbed
By my blood.

Lobotomies,
Phrenology,
Electric shock—

Listen
While you
Measure the

Limits of
The bull-
Pitted head.

Reoccurring,
The dream

In which
A hanged man

Wakes
& blows
Me a kiss.

For
The golden
Clothespin,

Scuff of
The sidewalk,
Hold

My hand
Before
It falls off.

Beneath
Streetlights,

Rats dance
Through

Chewed-
Open cans.

The fun
Park inside

Is being
Renovated.

Bellwether,
Blackened eyes.

Along
The interstate
Construction

Signs flash:
Warning.
Zombies

Ahead.
Run for
Your Lives!

The hours
Grow

Bloated
While I

Climb
The ladder.

Each rung
I touch

Bursts
Into flames.

If truth will
Never be
Known,

I regret
To inform you:
Fuchsia roses

Drying, upside
Down on
The clothesline.

The cat
Fur—

I collect
It in old

Spaghetti
Jars. She will

Never die.

The art
Of contemplation

Escapes me.
I'd rather

Be a missile
Filled
With honey.

Don't you
Worry

About
The sky

Pressing
Down with

Its never-
Wanting-to-be.

Night wind
Overturns

The lawn
Chairs.

A stranger
Is asleep

On the lawn.

Look in the eye of a chicken and you'll know.
— WERNER HERZOG

starved

In exchange for this buttery
Moment, I will try my best.

Then a bit more. For you
Are the dominatrix in

My head & this year
Should have been so different.

There has been an illness under
My bed. This life is just a boat

Bailing water. & even that
Doesn't matter anymore

Because it's all on fire.
Our weight shrews away.

Here, power comes to us
By fading. The inner part

Of ourselves. The small bones.
Olive oil syringed in the ear. It is

Damage. It is perfect. What does it
Mean to grace the lips of the dead?

O all of the things you will not let
Yourself see. Not a big feeler? Never sleep.

fancy beasts

Chickens dangle
From fishing rods
That hang over
The concrete ledge.
Clucking chum,
Spinning slowly
In the breeze. Every
Strange animal
In our cage
Waits for the dead
Goats to fall
From heaven.
Leaves switchback
Away from the sumac.
At dusk, men
& women can be
Seen swandiving
From the skyline.
Morning comes
& we toss our feces
Into the air.
Noon, we hold out
Our arms like a nailed-
Up Jesus or torture
Victims. It smells
Like mint & burnt

Lamb here, a piano
Left out in the rain.
For good luck,
Throw quarters
At our hooded heads.

house rulez

Information from
A reliable source
Leads us to believe
That an illegal dogfight
Has been taking place
In the cage of your skull
& after listening to the evidence
Pretended to them by
The prostitution, a jury
Of penises has found you
Guilty, guilty & more guilty!
Therefore, in accordance
With the powers vested
To me by the great state
Of Californication, I hereby
Sentence you to a lifetime
Of breeched labor within
The confines of your bored-out
Head. Son, you made your bed
& done gone & pissed in it!
So, wake up! Welcome
To the planet earth! & we got
Some regulations we'll gladly
Enforce, so listen here—
Lights out at ten.
Breakfast is never
Gonna be an omelet.

Don't look away from
The crackling sparks
Of your blowtorch
Unless your Santa suit
Catches fire. Only when
You smell sour
Turtle is it okay for you
To put out the flames.

the nice

All this time
I've crossed
My heart
With an X-Acto
Blade & water-
Boarded myself.
I am prepared
& I promise
I'm not hard
To puzzle
Whole with
The lights turned
Low. *Click, click,*
Poof, sleeping
Beauty. This is
The end of the road.
The four-star hotel
Is a car parked
In a puddle
Behind a supermarket.
Moonlight slicks
The boulevard's
Lilacs. Security lights,
Cameras, & thousands
Of pounds of antifungals

Surround us. But no one
Pays attention anymore.
The itching never stops.
Inside, the grinning face
On the milk carton
Has done more
In two dimensions
& black & white
Than it could fathom
Before he vanished
From the play-
Ground. Write it
In the steamed-up
Windshield. I am not
Here to be the king
Of July Fourth.
I am weathering
This endless midnight
Inside a corona
Of sparklers, until

The past finally
Stutter-steps out
Of itself. For a limited
Time & just for you,
I promise. & when
We get there,

We'll forever walk
The aisles, chins
Raised to the humming
Fluorescents. Our shrouds
Lifting like bouquets.

come get some

The August sky is a blister
pack of muscle relaxers

& my bones regret everything
I've done. Ache. Ack. Arse.

There's no question I've outlasted
my usefulness, so adios. Peace

out. All night I pace back & forth
in front of the police station,

practicing my better living. I'm trying
to live off of the grid—recycling

myself & eating fingernails. I've got
a collection of fedoras made from

dead skin & hair. It's your last
chance—tomorrow, between noon

& noon-thirty, I'll be in the parking lot
of the Salvation Army. Come on—

be there—I've got a truckload
of pharmacy-grade stardust & light.

Now! Right now! Everything must go!

modern life

The pickup that's slammed
Into my garbage bins each
Tuesday night the last three

Weeks does it again tonight
While I watch from the living-
Room window. Last time I wrote

Down the license-plate number,
But each day, when I pick up
The phone to call the cops, the name

Of the song I'd been all morning
Trying to remember cottons my mouth.
For a year, there's been a pain

Arrowing up my spine, squatting
Behind my eyes. Doctors scratch
Their chins & scribble more

Prescriptions. Trash flutters through the street.
Bolts of street-lamp light outline
The plastic bags that tumble across my lawn.

The pickup screeches through the stop sign
At the end of the block & swerves around
The corner. The tires squawk & the frame leaps

Forward. Little mouths of flame, the taillights
Swing away. When I was young, I'd lie face down
In bed, & eyes closed see a keening cloud

Pull up from my body & rise through
The ceiling. I was illuminated from inside.
Now the simplest wind, just a ripple, smells

Tartly medicinal. It feels like someone's
Been spitting tar into my mouth. I know that
Trouble—the driver's violent turning. The windshield

A black melt even though the headlights are on.
Thinking that none of it matters anyway
Because you'll be home soon, even

When the rain starts. I will not go out to clean
The mess of garbage up. Let the gusting storm
Pin it against the fence down the street. In the humid

Morning, wet newspapers will be lacquered
To the sidewalk. The orchestra of house finches
Tearing it apart will look up when I step

Onto the porch. They'll stare blankly, willing
Me to understand how empty the feeders are.
That the birdbath is once again filled with shit.

How do they keep at it like this? All that jabbering,
When just breathing the humid air feels like drowning.
There are so many good things in life I've overlooked.

we could
boom boom

Saying yes to everything
Does not mean you need

To grunt at each person
Who says hello. I have

Taken this to heart.
When my mind is

A colander beaded
With mercury,

I name the world
RIDING A BIKE

WITH NO LEGS. I look
Into each passerby's eyes.

There have been quite a few
Moments when I've felt

Like I completely understood
The proper way to pounce

On a stranger from the deep
Shadows of a live oak,

But I never remember
What to do when I'm back

On the mealy ground.
Instead of bolting after,

Snatching the purse, I turn totem
Pole & stand like a jack-o'-lantern.

I've met many people who have died
This way. But I'm a lucky man.

Welcome, welcome. Yes, yes, yes.

erasure

How quickly we become
Nothing at all—hip bones

Gnawed by mutts after seasons
Of endless drizzle float them

Back up through the dirt. But even
In the flash that is before, *it is*

Immeasurable—this tiredness—
And only a blink to take everything

In. Heaps scattered through
The early-morning parking lot.

The blended light and air wafting
Thick with the just-opened donut

Shop. Whoever finds us will say
We were such small, stupid people—

Rain having worked lathelike
Upon our flattened skulls, bouquets

Of sunshine sprouting through
Our cavity-shadowed husks.

the big one

Forehead sweat pearled,
And then down, turning

Tiny circles on the table, you
Laugh-sputter, about to give

Up on what's left of the four-
And-a-half-pound rib eye

In front of you. The last thing
You remember tasting

Were your tears, and they caught
In your throat like marbles

Of honey. The threadbare bandanna
You wear over your face like a robber's

Is all BBQ sauce. Who actually had
Faith you could put it all down,

Anyway? Who was it that told you to eat
That trough of fried okra? So often

Your hours cut apart like this—chin
Left shining with grease, stomach

A ratty mattress squashed
To the size of a tennis ball.

Each of our days, you've always
Been told by the people who love

You, has somewhere in its unfolding
Ticks the potential to be the best one

Ever—record shattering. A tock that makes
The floorboard buckle. But it's so hard

To hold all of those wonderful possibilities
Inside you right now—that wreath

Of gristle you dropped down your throat.
How you tipped back, opening your face

Like a boa constrictor to drop the flag
Of fat in. And so you slump backward, trying

To breathe—hoping for the miraculous
Puff of one more inch of emptiness. For a dark

Pocket to appear in your belly—hollow
And ready for more. Water-filled plastic baggies

Dangle and twist like translucent stomachs
From the ceiling cracks they've been nailed into,

Refracting the day's stooped light.
The restaurant whirls around you

Like a mirror ball, and two flies bang
Ecstatically against your lip's sweet tar. What was,

For the briefest moment, an orchestral
Shifting inside you soon sounds like an armchair

Scraped across a hardwood floor. The heart heaving
Is so tremendous with joy, at first jolt, you cannot help it,

You smile and tighten your fork grip, twirling
The dulled knife as you prepare to dive in.

a little bit now

Bring kindness for it does not slice
 Us so

  The morning sun gasps
 & exposes the body's insides

We go fleafloored & vicious
 Darkly & the party is water

  All night we go into mouths
Fashionable with disease & pliable

  With forgetting we go
   Where each syllable is just

Out of reach Spun in the undeliverable

  Starlight— We go rushing

Ruined & headfirst we go Into the oven
  Hushing We go beveled

  About this grubby kingdom
Pressing our palms   To the river

Bottom   We go listing
     Into the unfathomable
               Canting with wondrous cruelty

cittern

I've been meaning. This holy roast
Banjoed in the skin of my chest.
This movement from day to night.
Water is a better guide than GPS,
Or the bullshit maps Google keeps
E-mailing me. I've been meaning
To sharpen the tools. A fresh
Coat of paint. Kick the tires.
I've been waiting. Wanting. I have
Been. To ask you about such
Things. I've been drinking too much
Water. Mercury in my gut.
I've been meaning to ask you
Why men fight so much. I know you
Want to blame it on the Chinese
Toy factories. I know you want
To go out tonight & find a body
Of water to sink into. Everything
In the living room has been wrapped
In maps. The moment has passed.
My new shoes have every future
Moment stitched into their soles
But I still don't know how
To leave you alone. Look into the beehive.
Your life is roadmapped out in front
Of you. All you have to do is get
There. You were born knowing

Everything. But like an old-school
Movie reel, it all rolled back into
One solid nothing. In today's
Leavening air, you don't even know
How to get underground.

the physics of sawing yourself in half

Because the cleanest cut is the best,
a band saw is the most efficient way
to peel a banana or ensure that the last
word spoken will be the last. How to separate
the self from the one thing the self knows?
Grim faced and happy, it does not & will
not ever completely know. Cleaving
& clinging & cleaving. Just like the backpack
slipped off the little boy's shoulder when the car
struck him, I slough off my skin & watch
it flutter behind me like a kite of my failings.
I creak along worrying about when the garbage
disposal will finally break down, & the shadow
of the floating shape is tireless through the park
below me. When I reach for it, I am, for the briefest time,
that which is all elbows & knees, that which is
the kid seldom seen. So I stand in the sun, smiling,
letting the downtown passersby stomp around
like starving cows. The day is a chafing wallet
& I seem to have forgotten my cattle prod
in a passed life & I had more than a bit
of trouble getting in these jeans. Ah to be
ice cream again. Straight up weed no angel
dust. All of the walkers' shoes singing out
in pain, those poor lowing cattle. I like my

burgers bunless & shaped into tiny pit bulls
that look like the one that attacked me the first
day of my job taking care of Eliot, the beautiful
boy with Down's syndrome. I avalanche ketchup
over it all & yodel. I punch my eyes & yawn.
Tomorrow if I wake up I'll spend the hours waving
into every window I'm lucky enough to stand in front of.

please please
more napalm

Are you having trouble
Remembering
Your birthday? How to spell
Dog? It's going to be
An interesting
Couple of lifetimes
Now that our genes
Have been blendered
From all of the chemicals
In our drinking water.
Each night I wander
Down the hallway
In the dark & drink
From the toilet & piss
In the fridge.
My best friend says
His nipples feel
Like bulldozers.
Another woke up
With a pound of
Opium hidden
In his ass. The ice
Caps melt. In line
At the supermarket
The lady in front of me

Jams a pen in the neck
Of the woman in front
Of her. The fields are
On fire. Everything
In the fish tank turns
Into a gelatinous block.
We wake from naps
With the collie staring
At us, wondering
Why we're wearing
Its collar. Ceramic angels
& dolls with roll-back
Eyes. It's either
A wet Baby Ruth
Or you shit the bed.
The wonks say that time is
Running out, so we gather
In a circle & pretend to care.
All those things we are
Never supposed to forget.
We hold hands, listening
To the trees wind-rip
Their litanies—cherries
& pecans, peaches.
Bluebirds fall
From the limbs.
Leaves pile. At night
Someone comes
To stitch them
Into eyeless masks.

operation:
get down

It is very
Common
    To have

A cave within us
    To hide

Away in when it all
Seems hopeless. To cry

    Tears of mostly blood.

To feed on the day-
    Dream in which

Side mirrors shear off
    Of your car

As the walled road
    Narrows.

To swerve might make…

There is a saint for the down
& out. A rock is a rock

Is a rock & redwood
Trees grow out
Of our chests.

It is horrible & right,
Here in this place. *Dum*

Spiro, spero. We're all in
This shit together.

dear dysentery

And when the piano drops
On you, it's like *wow,* this is all

There is? Plop, plop—fizz, fizz.
But because you've never been all

That good at telling time, you're early
& no one's there to let you in.

The note on the pearly gates says
Back in a Jiffy!—Now, You've Got Five

Seconds—Take Your Pick! & as you read,
You feel yourself being torn asunder

Because now you have a bit more
Dying to do. The stopwatch

In your chest counts down
As your options clarify in the air

In front of you—another pull
On the bungo juice or a leap

From the roof. That's all
There is. There's not even time

To bitch that it isn't fair—you've only got
Four seconds left & only now, just

Today, you found out that humpback
Whales can sing rhyming tunes

For twenty-two straight hours. Twenty-two goddamn
Hours! It's haunting how right

Everyone else has been—the monkey
On your back, the cake on the clown's nose—

From the gospel down to the extraordinary
Depth of Barry White's voice.

But you've known it from the beginning—
Those words lullabied to you by a nurse

The day after the day you shot your way out
Of the womb & burst into the world's
Pealing light—We are all

History & that's the way
The ball bounces, Little G.

all aboard

The small animals are having a dance
party all over me. A blowout.

There is about to be a three-second
violation on my belly. Firearms & tire

irons thrown into tire fires. Arms
rising like exclamation marks. Arms

piled like kindling. The knock-
down, the natural reaction. A good

old-fashioned gathering of fleas. Under
sweet & thrumming—get

perfect or decide that this can
only be it. Oh to go out like that.

Bang, bang. Pour it on. Hit
my reset. Let's start this shit over.

ABOUT THE AUTHOR

Alex Lemon is the author of the memoir *Happy* (Scribner, 2009) and of the poetry collections *Hallelujah Blackout* and *Mosquito*. The recipient of a fellowship from the National Endowment for the Arts, he teaches at Texas Christian University and lives in Fort Worth, Texas.

acknowledgments

These poems, sometimes in different parts, appeared in *Boulevard, Esquire, The Florida Review, Flurry, Fou, Harpur Palate, jubilat, Live Mag, Lo-Ball, The Los Angeles Review, The Mayo Review, The Offending Adam, Pleiades, Post Road, Quarterly West, The Southern Review, Third Coast, Typo Connotations, The Yale Younger Poets Anthology,* and *Whiskey Island.*

Thanks to the amazing folks at Milkweed, especially Jim Cihlar, and as always, love, love, love to all of my family and friends. I'm a lucky man.

more books from milkweed editions

To order books or for more information, contact
Milkweed at (800) 520-6455
or visit our Web site (www.milkweed.org).

Hallelujah Blackout
Alex Lemon

The Book of Props
Wayne Miller

Reading Novalis in Montana
Melissa Kwasny

Rooms and Their Airs
Jody Gladding

Music for Landing Planes By
Éireann Lorsung

Milkweed Editions

Founded in 1979, Milkweed Editions is one of the largest independent, nonprofit literary publishers in the United States. Milkweed publishes with the intention of making a humane impact on society, in the belief that good writing can transform the human heart and spirit.

Join Us

Milkweed depends on the generosity of foundations and individuals like you, in addition to the sales of its books. In an increasingly consolidated and bottom-line-driven publishing world, your support allows us to select and publish books on the basis of their literary quality and the depth of their message. Please visit our Web site (www.milkweed.org) or contact us at (800) 520-6455 to learn more about our donor program.

Milkweed Editions, a nonprofit publisher, gratefully acknowledges sustaining support from Amazon.com; Emilie and Henry Buchwald; the Patrick and Aimee Butler Foundation; the Dougherty Family Foundation; the Ecolab Foundation; the General Mills Foundation; John and Joanne Gordon; William and Jeanne Grandy; the Jerome Foundation; Robert and Stephanie Karon; the Lerner Foundation; Sally Macut; Sanders and Tasha Marvin; the McKnight Foundation; Mid-Continent Engineering; the Minnesota State Arts Board, through an appropriation by the Minnesota State Legislature, a grant from the Wells Fargo Foundation Minnesota, and a grant from the National Endowment for the Arts; Kelly Morrison and John Willoughby; the National Endowment for the Arts, and the American Reinvestment and Recovery Act; the Navarre Corporation; Ann and Doug Ness; Jörg and Angie Pierach; the RBC Foundation USA; Ellen Sturgis; the Target Foundation; the James R. Thorpe Foundation; the Travelers Foundation; Moira and John Turner; and Edward and Jenny Wahl.

Interior design and typesetting by Christian Fuenfhausen
Typeset in Fairfield LH Light
Printed on acid-free paper
by Friesens

ENVIRONMENTAL BENEFITS STATEMENT

Milkweed Editions saved the following resources by printing the pages of this book on chlorine free paper made with 100% post-consumer waste.

TREES	WATER	SOLID WASTE	GREENHOUSE GASES
9	**4,194**	**255**	**871**
FULLY GROWN	GALLONS	POUNDS	POUNDS

Calculations based on research by Environmental Defense and the Paper Task Force.
Manufactured at Friesens Corporation